Edwardian Teddington

Teddington High Street c1908 showing the premises of Ives the Butcher on the left hand side and Parr's Bank on the right. Photo courtesy of Howard Webb.

KEN HOWE was born and grew up in Teddington. He has always been interested in the history of Teddington and has written some books on the subject including "*Teddington Past and Present*" and "*Hampton and Teddington Past*" with John Sheaf. He is an active member of the History Research Group of The Teddington Society and a past chairman of the Borough of Twickenham Local History Society. He gained an MA in Local History from Kingston University. His other hobbies include real ale and rugby football. He is married and lives in Teddington with his wife Teresa and cat Sinbad.

EDWARDIAN TEDDINGTON

The Journal of Ellen "Nellie" Stocker nee Chitson (1895 - 1991)

Edited by Ken Howe

HISTORY INTO PRINT
56 Alcester Road,
Studley,
Warwickshire,
B80 7LG
www.history-into-print.com

Published by History Into Print 2010

A CIP catalogue record for this book is available from the British Library.

ISBN: 978-1-85858-338-9

Printed and bound in Great Britain by Information Press Ltd.

CONTENTS

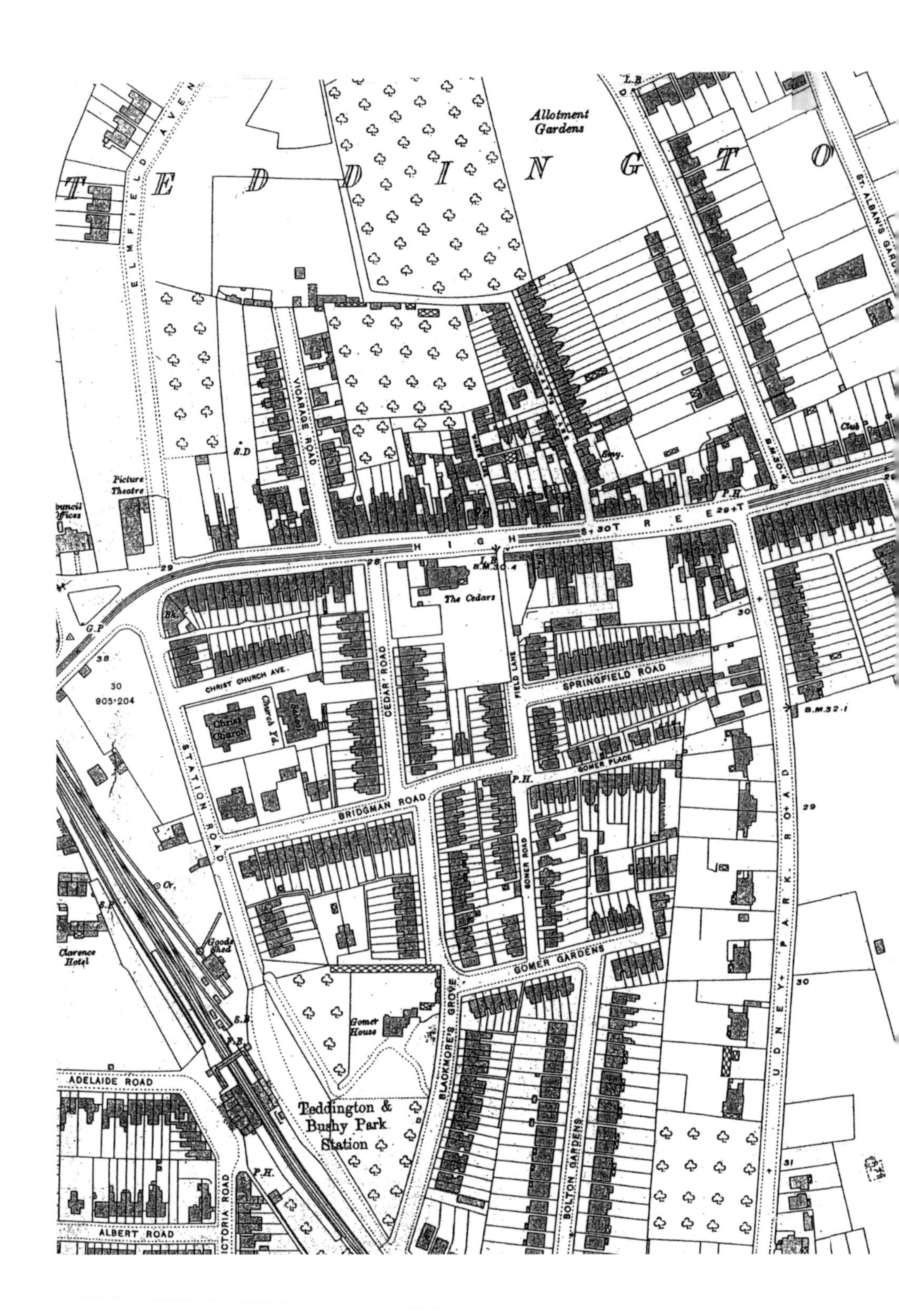

Allotment Gardens
T E D D I N G T O
Picture Theatre
The Cedars
S.D
HIGH STREET
L.B.
B.M.30·4
Bk.
G.P.
38
30
905·204
29
28
Club
Smy.
P.H.
VICARAGE ROAD
CHRIST CHURCH AVE.
Christ Church
Church Yd.
School
CEDAR ROAD
FIELD LANE
SPRINGFIELD ROAD
B.M.32·1
GOMER PLACE
BRIDGMAN ROAD
STATION ROAD
GOMER ROAD
GOMER GARDENS
Goods Shed
Clarence Hotel
Gomer House
BLACKMORE'S GROVE
Teddington & Bushy Park Station
ADELAIDE ROAD
ALBERT ROAD
BOLTON GARDENS
UDNEY PARK ROAD
31

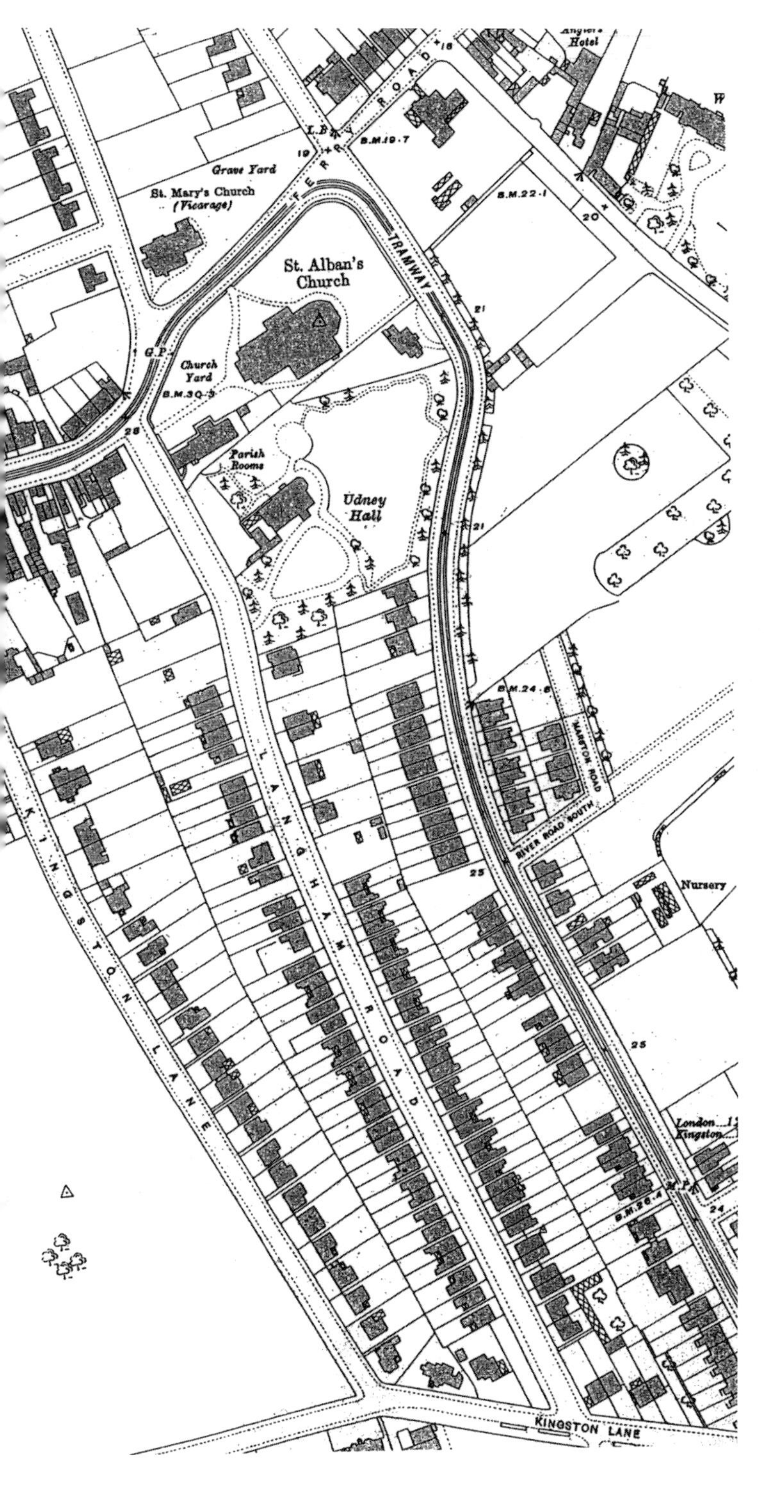

Map: 25" Ordnance Survey Map of Teddington 1915.

List of Illustrations

Acknowledgements

I AM GREATLY indebted to Jack Stocker for letting me use his mother's manuscript and for allowing it to be published, and also for providing some family photographs.

My thanks to Howard Webb for the cover photograph; to Richmond Local Studies Library for Figs 3, 4, 9, 17 & 27; to the City of London Picture Library for Fig 18. The other pictures are from the editor's own collection.

Also my thanks to Paddy Ching for checking my draft and providing some additional information.

Sources

THE MOST important source is Nellie Stocker's journal itself. Proper names have been checked and in some cases altered, against those listed in Kelly's Directories of 1905 and 1910. The Victoria County History of Middlesex section on Teddington, *Teddington As It Was, Teddington Past and Present* and *Hampton and Teddington Past* have all contributed to the text.

Foreword

I FIRST CAME to know Jack Stocker in 1997. He had been given one of my picture books on Teddington and being an ex-resident himself, he offered some additional information and some very amusing anecdotes.

As time passed on we grew to know each other better and I learned that Jack had been born in Teddington in 1921 and married and brought up his family here. He was working as manager at Sperry Gyroscopes, a firm of toolmakers in nearby Brentford, who in 1967 decided to take advantage of government relocation grants and establish a new factory in Bracknell. They wanted Jack to move with them and the lure of a new house whilst raising a young family eventually proved irresistible.

Despite having left Teddington in 1967, Jack still has fond memories of his home town and has given me several stories of his early life, which will be published shortly. I asked Jack what had prompted him to jot down his various tales and he told me he had been inspired by his mother, who, at the insistence of the family, had written the reminiscences of her early life in Teddington at the ripe old age of seventy seven.

Jack passed me a copy of her hand written journal which made absolutely fascinating reading. The detail in which she recalled each shop that she visited, her old school and everyday life in Teddington in 1905 was too good to ignore and Jack's story has had to be put to one side.

Ellen Annie or Nellie as she was called, was born into the Chitson family on December 11th 1895. The family came from Hoxton and in 1890, via a short spell in Hampton Wick, they settled in Teddington, living in Park Lane, Middle Lane, North Lane and Wades Lane. Her father, George Joseph Chitson, was a plumber, working across the River Thames at Ham. Her mother, Alice was at home, raising a family of eight children, Laura in 1889, Ethel in 1891, George in 1893, Ellen in 1895, Alice in 1897, Robert in 1900, Sidney in 1902 and Arthur in 1905.

Nellie went to Collis School and was a good pupil, winning six book prizes during her time there:

A Forgotten Christmas by Mrs Beames for Attendance 1904
The Luck of the Eardleys by Sheila E Braine for Domestic Economy 1906
Girl Neighbours by Sarah Tyler for Writing
Eighteen Stories for Girls by Lady William Lennox et al, 1st Prize 1907/8
Kitty Montgomery by A E Deane, 2nd Prize 1909
Little Hazel, the King's Messenger by the Author of "*Under the Oaks*" *1906*
Mrs Beeton's Cookery Book

In 1908 the Chitsons made their final move to 15 Bridgeman Road and it was to be from here that Nellie later married.

When she left school, she went to work for Phelps Furnishers in the Broad Street. She married Tom on 15th September 1915 at Kingston Registry and they lived in New Malden until 1917, when they moved to 44 Field Lane, Teddington. They had two sons, Walter and Jack. In 1965 they moved to 22 Field Lane where they stayed until Tom died on 28th October 1969, aged eighty three. Nellie and her eldest son, Walter moved to Binfield, Berkshire in 1982 to be closer to Jack and his family and Walter pre-deceased his mother and died on 15th August 1988, aged eighty-four.

Nellie, herself, eventually went into Birdsgrove Nursing Home where she died on 28th December 1991, aged ninety-six.

She lived through some very troubled times and was always in a position very near the poverty line until her later days but throughout these times, she bore her lot with fortitude and a cheerful sense of well-being, not complaining and always ready to offer a helping hand to whosoever needed it.

She also managed to write some poems which seem to very much reflect her feelings on life and three of them, all untitled, are shown at the back.

So here then in her own words is her story. I hope this work does her justice.

Ken Howe, Teddington, July 2010

PART ONE

Just a walk down Memory Lane in 1972

I AM SEVENTY seven years old and one of a family of eight, four sons and four daughters. There are only four of us left now though and we have a great affection for our hometown and we never tire of talking about the old times. Not that they were all good for we saw many lean times.

My father I think was born in Hampton Wick and went to the old school which has just been demolished. *[Nellie was wrong here although she did not know it at the time; her father was born in Hoxton on 15th May 1865 and did not move to Teddington until 1890]*. He met my mother when she was in service at "***Lyndhurst***" in Kingston Road. My mother's home was at Wooburn Green in Buckinghamshire and they were married at old Wooburn Church about 1886 *[in fact they married on Christmas Day 25th December 1888]* and they must have come to Teddington to live as my father worked at Ham. He was a plumber and worked for a man who had a house and yard on Ham Common; the house is still there. My father was called "***The Plumber***" by the inhabitants; he was well known and always had a joke ready and the population was so small, they all knew George Chitson the Plumber. *[Jack later confirmed that George Joseph Chitson was apprenticed as a plumber at a business in Ham. He was especially skilled in sheet lead work and worked on the building of several large houses. He also made his own oak furniture; the cabinets had doors carved to look like draped curtains,* *similar to those he had seen at Hampton Court Palace, but his main hobby was making scale models of famous buildings].*

He worked at practically all of the historical houses in Ham and Ham House in particular, home to the Dysarts, could tell many tales of his work.

Fig 1 *Ham House – Home of the Dysart family and now in the National Trust.*

I visited there last year *(1971)* and going round in a chair, I could point out much of the lead work on the roofs my father talked of. So much of the work on the large houses was lead in those days and my father was a masterpiece with lead. He started work each day at 6.00am and walked to and from work across Ham fields, which in those days were cultivated with corn or vegetables. *[In later life, George Joseph loved to boast that when walking down the driveway of Ham House, a horse and carriage would be coming towards him; it was Earl Dysart and he stopped the carriage and spoke to him. He was also on good terms with Admiral Fisher and Lord Beaufort, on whose houses he had worked].*

I was born in Middle Lane *[although the Chitsons were in Middle Lane in 1892, Nellie was born around the corner at 3 Rose Villas, North Lane]* but we must have moved to Wades Lane when I was very young for I started school at four years old and can still remember being in the babies' class and my teacher was Miss Batham. The school much improved as years went on. When in the first class, the babies' class it was called, I so well remember the seats went up in rows.

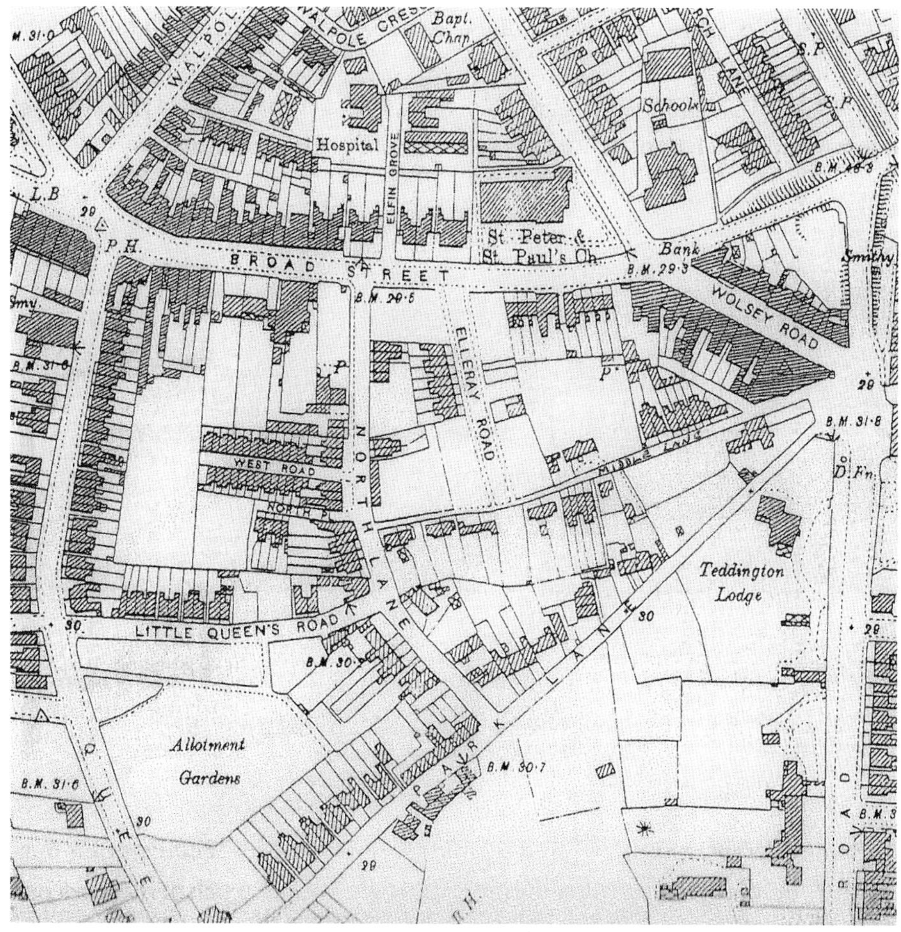

Fig 2 *Ordnance Survey Map of 1915 showing Middle Lane/North Lane.*

The teacher in front of the class could see you all clearly. One instance stands out in my mind was when I was being taken to school, being knocked down by a bicycle crossing (the High Street) from Wades Lane to Field Lane. The entrance for seniors was in Bridgeman Road and for juniors in Station Road in the alley the side of Christ Church. This was a mixed school but boys left at a certain age and went to St Mary's and St Peter's. Miss Sarah Collis was headmistress and in later years Miss May Collis her sister took over. My eldest sister, Laura, was in service with them and they lived in Victoria Road. She was very happy with them. *[May Collis was actually the niece of Sarah Collis but it was commonly assumed that they were sisters. The school was originally Station Road Day School for Girls and Infants in 1865, and renamed Christ Church School but such was*

Fig 3 *Collis School c1908 for girls and infants.*

the renown and reputation of the Collis family that it was recalled Collis School. The old building is still standing and is now an infants' playschool. A new Collis School was built in Fairfax Road in 1972].

I so very well remember when the school thought we should have a little more sport and can see us in the playground organised by the teacher playing such games as ***"Poor Ginny is a Weeping"***. What we would have given for a good game of ball but children were not so boisterous in those days. What a to-do when 24th May was here *[Empire Day, but renamed Commonwealth Day in 1952 for the coronation of Queen Elizabeth II]*. We had the flag flying in the playground and all had to go dressed in white if possible and we marched around and saluted the flag and sang a patriotic song; I can still sing ***"What is the Meaning of Empire Day"***. How things have changed.

Although we never had a lot of money to spend we were so much more content. We paid 2d a week for school money. If any were better off and could afford more, they could do so and their names went into a special book. Each year we had a prize giving and I remember such people as Mr Buckmaster were invited. I still have prizes which I am proud of. Mr Buckmaster at one time tried to encourage saving and presented a number of children with a Post Office book with 2/6d *(12p today)* deposited. I was lucky enough to have one but I just can't remember what happened about it; whether I saved but I've never had more than a few pounds in the PO, so I don't fancy it made me save. *[Nellie won seven book prizes between 1904 to 1909. J C Buckmaster was a well known local worthy. He was a local magistrate and councillor, laid the foundation stone to the library and encouraged thrift and education in every way].*

Fig 4 *John Charles Buckmaster JP.*

Our house in Wades lane was "***Pine Cottage***", it was very old. It backed on to Ive's the butchers on the High Street. The windows were all in front with a square of land in the front about 8 yards square, a door with top glass panels led into the kitchen (the door was the only light in that room) with the old fashioned open stove, big black kettles and pots. The stairs went up from that room and a door led into the sitting room and we had two bedrooms. We had a scullery, toilet and coal cellar outside. My father put up a lean-to from the door to the scullery, which was about 2 yards square with stone coffer and sink. A huge water butt was outside as rainwater was always preserved and used a lot then. Most people had a water butt. *[*Pine Cottage *was the first house on the right hand side from the High Street and that side was redeveloped in the 1950s. It is now difficult to follow the line of fields and back gardens that existed in 1905 but the gardens to* Shambles Wine Bar *must have been where Ive kept his livestock].*

We had only oil lamp and candles to light you to bed. The oil lamp - I can see it now, was brass and was carried into the sitting room on Sundays. We had an old fashioned harmonium, which came from Collis School when they had a new one - my father bought it cheap. He would play and we would sing hymns. We were not a religious family but we always respected Sunday and were made to go to Sunday school and Church. Our Sunday School was held in a large corrugated shed at the back of the shops in the High Street (where the Telephone Exchange is now) *[this was also the site of Bridgeman House, the home of Sir Orlando Bridgeman — the Keeper of the Great Seal at the time of the Restoration and buried in St Mary's Church]* and then we marched down to the Church for the service. After Church we dawdled around and I was always fascinated somehow by St Mary's churchyard and one thing that intrigued me was the tiny pansies, which grew wild around the graves. The graves were all very old but one family I knew had a grave there - a brother and sister named Tilbury and they were buried there. They lived in a cottage next to the *King's Arms.*

An alley that led to our house from the lane, which was also a back entrance to Stacey the Chemists. At the bottom of the alley lived the Overtons. Mr Overton was the cowman for Mr Edwin G Ive the butcher. I will tell you more about him when we get into the High Street later for I can't get away from Wades Lane at the moment. Let me take you into the lane from the High Street; on the right corner was a sweet shop owned by Mr & Mrs Glue. They had two daughters and a son (Mrs Glue was the daughter of the licensee of *The King's Arms,* Mr Barnes). Past the side entrance to some of the shops, there was a shed, which was a small sweet factory. I can't remember their name but we never thought a lot of the smell when toffee was cooking, (I can still remember though the taste of "Kalibonters" and "Sticky Toffee" and "Mackintosh Slab Toffee" sold at Glues.

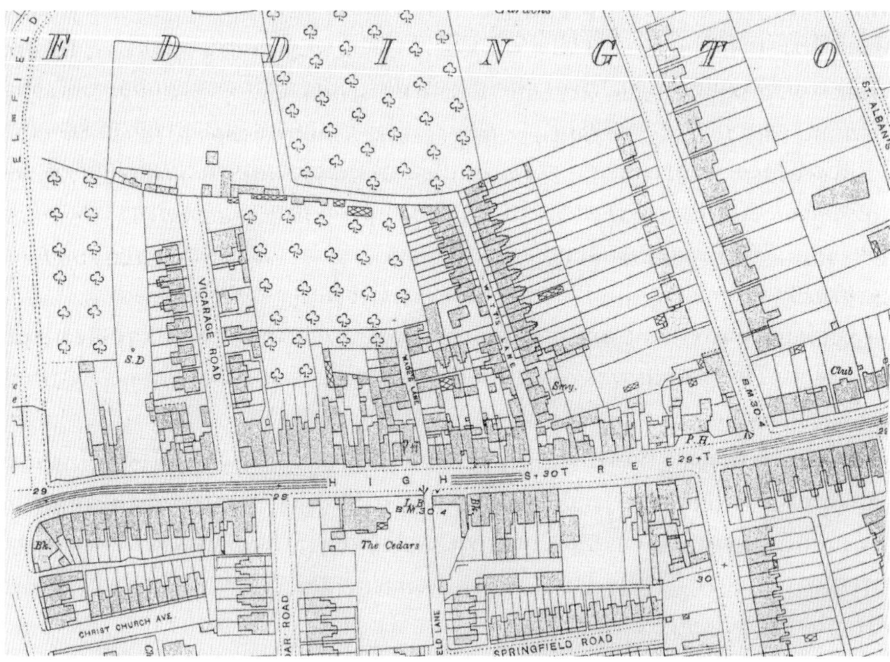

Fig 5 *Ordnance Survey Map 1915 of the High Street showing Wades Lane, Watts Lane and the surrounding lanes.*

Beyond his factory an entrance to two small cottages occupied by families Maysh and Rossen – they were related to each other; a little further was a blacksmiths, Mr Batham and his man. I spent many hours before I was old enough to go to school. Those beautiful big horses – I can see them now. If I got in the way the man would sit me on the horse while he was shod and I would have to stay there out of the way on his back 'till they thought fit to lift me down. I watched them make the shoes and put them on. I spent hours picking up the little spiky ends cut off the nails that held the shoe on and the little square ends cut off the ends of the shoes after they were made. I soon stopped that though when I picked up a hot one. I dropped it and ran and never told a soul although I suffered for I knew I'd be stopped going in there. As I got older I'd take them a cup of tea from my mum and they would let me work the bellows.

Beyond the blacksmith was Overton's Cottage. I have often wondered what that was originally used for, for it was a low wooden house and as you stepped in the door very low (slate floor) a room about 4 yards square. I often think it could have been a dairy for this room was called *"The Place"* and as all the boys grew up it was a boxing room and anything in the way of sports. On from there, three more houses and the end one, Smith's and his lovely orchard beyond. I can imagine the beautiful Victoria Plum and Golden Knob apples no bigger than a golf ball but the sweetest you ever tasted. Going in the gate to the orchard was a dog kennel and the dog on a lead long enough to reach anyone, I can see Elsie Smith saying "Come on, he won't hurt you" but I wouldn't move until she sent him into the kennel and sat in the hole till I passed. Up the path which was all fruit trees, at the end a long row of greenhouses with tomatoes and cucumbers and on past them to the most beautiful mulberries on fresh green mulberry leaves waiting to be delivered to the gentry in Manor Road, Broom Road etc. *[Part of the Smith's orchard was used for the swimming baths, opened in 1931 and the surrounding play ground].*

Then the potting sheds and more glass houses and then round the corner along a high wall which is now the swimming baths, to the end and round the corner and the garden at the back of the houses which have shops built in front of them, in the High Street. Out of the orchard then a row of about six houses and not very small houses.

If I remember rightly they were two storeys and are still there. I do know one at least has been modernised. Then we come to the slaughter house of Mr E G

Ive, the butcher in the High Street. Very high black building with slats high up for ventilation; this is where the animals were slaughtered. Just inside the gate was the pig sty on the left, then a big square concrete two feet high where the entrails were emptied and collected every so often (I can't say what for but they went). Then the stables and carts used to deliver the meat to the gentry. Just two wheel high carts were used in those days, and to the right into the slaughterhouse.

When the animals were brought up the lane, often in the winter when it was dark, the animals would go berserk and run anywhere, some say they smelled blood but many times they were up the alley and in our garden. We had bullocks and sheep at different times and what a job to get them out the cowman had and what a mess our garden was the next day too.

Further on down the lane the side entrance to *The King's Arms*, the bottle shed etc, the bars with sawdust on the floor and wooden stools and spittoons. There was a taproom where a club could be held. *The King's Arms* was then a beer house; no spirits sold and they kept open all day. *[Beer houses were licensed under the Beer Act of 1830 and permitted the sale of beer, ale and cider only. This was a Government way of deferring the sale of gin which occurred in inns and taverns.* The King's Arms *became a beer house about 1860 and obtained a full licence much later. Most beer houses operated loan clubs or Christmas clubs which were organised and run by the clientele].*

I spent many hours in there, as the granddaughters Edie and Lily Glue were my friends. Lily is married and lives at Hounslow now and Edith is still alive but a sick woman. Later as Mr Barnes got old, his son Harry and his wife came there to live.

Well as I said I will go to the left past the sweet shop owned by Mr & Mrs Glue. I can still imagine the happy times then, when we had a party. Next door was a tailor and then a drapers. Then a barbers shop, an opening with steps up to Stacey's House. They had the chemist's shop and it's still there. *[It was in 1972 but closed soon after and became first an antiques shop and second, Pinocchio's Gift Shop].*

Then E G Ive – a fine big man with one son Ted and two daughters, Lizzie and May. Ted later took over the shop after his father, and Lizzie was on the desk. May married into an old Teddington family who had their own farm – the Holdaway family. Lizzie eventually married Wintour Phelps and had two

Fig 6 *High Street.*

daughters and after her husband died, she came back to the shop and when Ted retired she went abroad to her daughter. *[When Ted retired, the trade continued as Stapleton's the Butchers and in the 1970s it became* Shambles Wine Bar, *retaining many of the original features of the butcher's shop. Wintour Phelps was a successful businessman; having a department store in Broad Street on the site of the present Tesco's where Nellie was to start work later].*

Fig 7 *Broad Street showing Wintour Phelps department store.*

Back to E G Ive days though, he really did have the most beautiful meat. All home killed and at Christmas, his animals always won prizes and he had them on show for about two weeks before Christmas and were then killed and the huge great prize sides of beef and pork hung up and outside the shop each with rosettes and prize badges. It would do us all good to get meat like it now. I know what beautiful dripping even the ran-down fat made. That was one that we always had in our house – a good basin of dripping. *[Dripping was part of the staple diet of the day and very popular]*.

Next to Ive's, Chester the decorator, and then Tozer's the baker, all bread and cakes cooked on the premises. This is the corner of Watts Lane. This again has seen many changes for up on the left lived an old Teddington family – the Tates. The sons were postmen – such a well-respected family. Mrs Tate a real rosy-faced woman was paid by St Albans Church to open a soup kitchen, and Tuesdays and Thursdays were soup days and beautiful pea soup it was too with meat from Ives the butcher. We used to go with our quart jugs after we came out of school lunchtime. I think if I remember right it was 1½d a quart. I expect that price sounds ridiculous now but a man's wages were so small and prices had to cope. We were much better off than some for my father had a trade.

On up Watts Lane; Tozer's Oar and Scull Makers – two of my brothers were apprenticed there and they made all by hand. My brothers used to make models at home so I saw how they were made. One oar or scull was made out of one single piece of wood, all done with plane, spoke shave and sandpaper. They made sculls for the Oxford and Cambridge crews and my brother, Arthur, went for a time to Putney to work for Phelps who had so much to do with the crews.

Going up Watts Lane from the High Street, on the right side were a greengrocer, Mrs Mayhew and her daughter and up the lane the last few houses, the last two to my knowledge were very low houses – no upstairs. I had a friend and her widowed mother lived in one and out the back was a square, no garden cultivated and along one side a toilet for each house. My friend had to walk across the yard to the corner to theirs. Later this became a blacksmith's shop owned by Moscrop. *[The Moscrop family was a well known Teddington family who were involved in various businesses]*.

In the High Street past the greengrocers was a toyshop, Mr Cleak. *[Cyril Cleak is actually listed in Kelly's Directory as a Stationer]*. He did quite a good trade for

Fig 8 *Beaney Boot Shop in the High Street.*

there was no other unless you went over the bridge. Next was the fishmonger's, Mr Burtenshaw has it now and I always remember it as a fish shop but I can't remember the name of who owned it. *[It was probably Walter Preece].* Next was an undertaker – Porters. This was later a joiners and then an engineering shop. Not too much interest until we get to the last shop before *The King's Head*, which was Beaney's the boot shop, another well-known Teddington family.

The King's Head has now been rebuilt but when I first remember it, it was owned by Mr Ridgen and his son and daughter. [The King's Head *was originally established in 1668 and is one of the oldest pubs in Teddington. The last Court Leet was held here before power was handed over to the Parish Vestry. At the time of writing, the pub is undergoing conversion to a gastro-pub operated by the restaurateur, Raymond Blanc].* My father knew most of the

Fig 9 *King's Head Public House.*

publicans that were handy because all the (beer) pipes were lead in those days and he was often called to see to them. The side of *The King's Head*, if I remember rightly was a cab place. No cars at all at that time, all carriages and at weddings the beautiful grey horses, if you had the money to pay for them.

The first big house on the other side of Cambridge Road, steps up to the front door, was Mr Tate the dentist. I had my first tooth out there. No gas in those days - he injected something but I thought he was pulling my head off. He patted me on the shoulder and told me I was a good girl. I guess I was about 14 years old. I can still imagine it now. The row of houses is still there - Oxford and Cambridge Villas. Then on further, on the corner opposite, was a well known corn chandler - Mr Metcalf, he had stables and a shop. Then Peg Woffington's Cottages - in those days most picturesque all covered in wisteria. On the corner around the bend was Manor Road. *[Although called Peg Woffington Cottages and bearing the date plaque of 1754, there is no evidence that she actually built these cottages as almshouses for the poor of Teddington, as tradition would have it].*

Fig 10 *Peg Woffington Cottages.*

Unfortunately there is a gap in the journal which suggests that Nellie was saying something about Manor Road and maybe the Manor House but we can only guess at what might have been written.

On the opposite corner St Mary's Church. I have no need to enlarge on that for it was always even in my young days very old and as I said before, I only remember the Tilbury family being buried there. *[Despite strong Saxon*

Fig 11 *St Mary's Church.*

connections, the earliest date for a church here is 1217 although the present building is clearly much later. There was certainly a church here prior to the conquest when the Manor of Teddington was administered by Westminster Abbey].

Then to Ferry Road. More nice houses in those days owned by people with money to spare, as we would say then, the Rich. At the end in later years a laundry called the Riverside Laundry sprang up and employed quite a few women. I knew several who worked there.

Then the boathouses and workshops owned by Sims, a very well known family in the boat world,

Fig 12 *Ferry Road.*

and on the opposite side of the road beside *The Anglers* way down to the river was Burgoyne and Bunn, another well-known Teddington firm. *[As far as I have been able to trace, Burgoyne's yards were at Kingston and Hampton Wick but their boats must have come through Teddington Lock. Tom Bunn's yard was definitely at Teddington and operated from about 1905 to 1925].* On a Sunday the river there would be crowded with boats. People came up the river (or was it down), tied up their boats (always a man there to help them) and went to *The Anglers* for a drink. In those days the river was always in use and at weekends, crowded with pleasure punts, skiffs and rowing boats. These could be hired from both

Fig 13 *The Anglers Public House.*

firms and it was one of the most popular pastimes and at weekends especially, the river was crowded. So many would row up to Eel Pie Island where they catered for fun and refreshment or to Richmond where the crowds would find so much to amuse them and the beautiful scenery. The view from Richmond Hill across the river is still a most beautiful picture.

Pleasure steamers were always plying between Richmond and Hampton Court and had to come through Teddington Lock. This again was a sight on Sunday mornings and evenings to help push and open the locks which was opened by a long tubular pole about two feet in diameter. This attached to the bridge across the lock and opened when the lock was filled or emptied whichever the case was needed. Sunday evenings the lock was filled to capacity with perhaps a pleasure steamer and as many small boats as possible crammed in. *[The first lock built here was in 1811 and at that time, Teddington was*

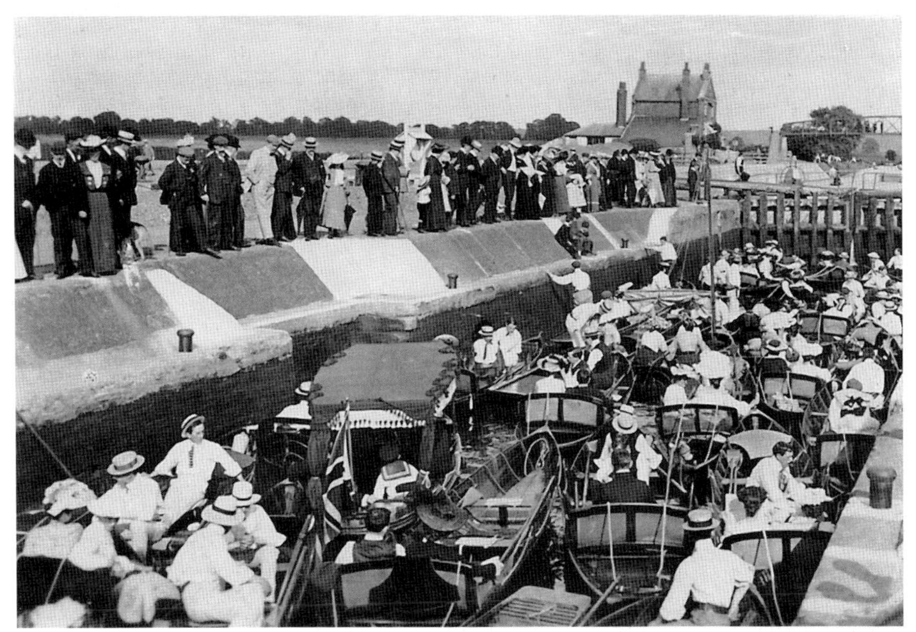

Fig 14 *Teddington Lock.*

the last lock on the Thames until Richmond half-lock was opened. It still marks the end of the tidal stretch of the river. A cut into the land on the Surrey bank was made to create the lock. Navigation was much improved and the busy use of the lock caused it to be rebuilt in 1858 and at this time, a skiff or "coffin" lock was added for the use of small craft. A boat slide for canoes was also fitted in 1863. Finally the great barge lock was built in 1904].

Leaving the locks, it was always a very pleasant walk to Richmond or Kingston along the towpath with anglers sitting so patiently on the bank or a walk across Ham Fields and a drink perhaps at the ***Crooked Billet, the Hand in Flower*** or the ***New Inn*** before walking through the woods surrounding Ham House to Petersham. You could look through the tall iron gates at Ham House and the beautiful grounds.

We leave the water and coming back past the very old cottages and one in the middle was turned into a pub – ***The Monkey House*** it was called in the early days and then ***The Cottage Inn*** and then ***The Tide End Cottage*** and then a couple

Fig 15 *Tide End Cottage Public House.*

of cottages and Broom Road. Just around the corner ***The Anglers Hotel*** and on the opposite corner was all land belonging to the big houses in Broom Road. Houses with plenty of servants and they had their own coachmen and coach houses. I can remember two on the land opposite the houses and one always had a clock built in, which could be seen when passing St Alban's Church.

This was always thought a beautiful church and when Rev Boyd was vicar, he had high hopes of it being a cathedral and did his best to raise money for the purpose but it was never completed. *[Rev Francis Leith Boyd was a very ambitious priest and came to Teddington in 1884. Having observed the population of Teddington increasing from 1,180 in 1861 to 6,600 in 1881, he realised that St Mary's Church would not be big enough to house the larger congregation and set about building St Alban's, which opened still unfinished in 1889. Its green copper roof was a useful landmark for miles around].*

I so well remember on St Alban's day the clergy and choir led a procession along the High Street in their surpluses and robes and it was the same every year. The Kensits, a religious body, always came down from London and caused

Fig 16 *St Alban's Church.*

Fig 17 *The Kensits, separated from the St Albans Procession by a strong police contingent. The parade is passing the Kings Head with Beaney's Boot Shop on the left and the new cab firm in the courtyard of the pub.*

disturbances and tried to break up the processions. I think it was opposing the church becoming high church. Of course as children we always thought it fun and everyone turned out to see what happened. *[The Kensit Wickliffe Preachers were established in 1899 by John Kensit to oppose the Oxford Movement which was dedicated to taking the Church of England back to its Pre-Reformation state i.e. part of the Church of Rome. From 1907 until the end of the Great War, they demonstrated with varying degrees against any move towards Roman Catholicism and in particular at the Teddington St Alban's Festival day which sometimes ended in violence and bloodshed.]*

Langham Road comes next after walking around the churchyard. On the opposite corner of Langham Road, the adult school, run by St Alban's Church. I remember in later years when I married, my husband told me it was a club to encourage lads; there was sport such as billiards but they had to make so many attendances to be a member. From what I gather, they had some fun too. *[This building was Feversham House, named after Sir Anthony Feversham, nephew of Charles Duncombe, banker and Lord Mayor of London at Teddington Place and one of the richest men in England, and saw many different uses in its life. It was a school run by Miss Acton for fifty years and from 1911 until it was demolished in 1918, it was the St Albans Club].*

Fig 18 *Sketch of Feversham House.*

Next some very old cottages standing back in their front gardens. Then an opening up to the house and stables of Pomfretts who owned carriages for hire.

Then Morgan's the sweet shop. My favourite in there if I had a copper on the way home from church was "Violet Gums", I think they were made by Rowntree and they were much smaller than any other gums I've ever seen. Some mauve and some clear and the most beautiful flavours, the shape of a little tiny pudding, they were expensive too – 1d an ounce. The sweets in those days were 4ozs and 8ozs a 1d, and ½d would buy many varieties. When I think of the large pear drops my mother and father sometimes went to Kingston on a Saturday evening and he used to bring 1 lb of them. I think they were 3d a pound.

Then the *Royal Oak;* that was such a low old place with a porch over the main door and one had to pass under or get into the road to pass. The windows of the bar were so low we sat on the sills as children and could look into the windows. *[At this time the* Royal Oak *was built on the roadside and a proposed plan to build a road bridge over Teddington Lock caused the pub to be knocked down and rebuilt further back from the road, creating a car park in front. The plan never materialised but the pub was rebuilt. Time has now gone full cycle and the site has been developed again and brought the* Oak, *lately renamed* Sammy's *back to the pavement].*

Fig 19 *The High Street with the Royal Oak on the left hand side.*

Then the main and the only one on the High Street side of the bridge, the corn chandler – Mr Metcalf. He sold everything for animals and at the back, bales of hay and straw for horses. He owned a big cart and lovely big horses.

The next block of flats from Kingston Lane to Udney Park were built when I was quite young *(Grand Parade built 1900).* I so remember going with my sister to collect bits of wood for the fire, along the back alley way and often being chased by Mr Andrews, the old man who was the watchman. All the shops in the front of these flats have changed hands repeatedly during all the years.

The shop that stands out in my mind was Lemons the baker. He was the high class baker and his cakes etc were more fancy and more pricey too. The only time we could be lucky if we could get 2d of stale cakes. He did quite a lot of catering. His shop, if only I had a picture of it, (was) very picturesque and again very low - you stepped down as you went in and a Miss William was the chief one in the shop, right through their stay in the shop and still when they retired, she went with them.

Fig 20 *Lemons the Bakers.*

Then the cycle shop run by Mr Stockwell and a flight of steps up to his shop. Mr Stockwell only had one leg and a crutch. My sister and I used to hire a cycle at 3d an hour and he carried these up and down the steps so easily. The rough roads and no cars, there used (to be) cycles ridden by most people who had to travel to work. I remember when I started work, my brother and I brought a new bike and had to pay instalments for it. We bought "Swift" bikes and Mr Stockwell's shop was then nearer to the bridge, almost opposite where the Post Office is now. *[The present shops there are low floored and the steps leading up from the pavement are still there].*

Then there was a tall building, it was a club and Mr Stamp and his wife were the caretakers and there was a corrugated building at the back where we went to Sunday School. *[This was Bridgeman House, reputedly the home of Sir Orlando Bridgeman or at least on the site of it. It became the St Albans Club where members played billiards and chess. R D Blackmore was a frequent visitor. It was demolished in the 1950s to make way for the Telephone Exchange]*. Then Coleman and his sons, butchers and a grocer Norrish and then we had a drapers shop (two shops together) Russells, then Millests the bakers. A very big man and he was so well remembered for his awful language. He used to frighten me. He never kept his staff very long. Then Pouparts the dairy, then a jewellers. Next the "***White House***", the Doctors' House. We had Doctors Coalbank, Davidson and Camps practising there. Dr Coalbank and his family lived in Park Road. *[They were in Teddington Lodge which was demolished for the Police Station. The* "White House" *remained in commercial use until 2008 when it was demolished to make room for a block of flats and a Starbucks Coffee Shop]*.

Fig 21 *Pouparts the Dairy.*

Dr Davidson lived in one of the tall houses down by the river (in) Ferry Road. Dr Camps lived at the ***White House*** and later in Udney Cottage, Kingston Lane, specialised in ears, nose and throat. Dr Camps' son was, in later years, Francis Camps the Pathologist, who recently died. Dr Coalbanks' son took over the practice of his father after his death.

The oldest doctor I remember was Dr Clarke (my father's doctor) and Dr Austin who was always *(allegedly)* drunk. He was Medical Officer of Health. Dr Poole too was a very clever and ... *(the sentence was left unfinished).*

The opposite corner of Field Lane was "***The Cedars***", a big house in its own grounds extending from Field Lane to Cedar Road and many years previously had covered the whole square taking in Bridgeman Road. A high Roman wall surrounded it leaving Field Lane a narrow country lane overhanging with beautiful trees and on the other side, the grounds of *"The White House"*. This corner holds one special memory for an ice cream barrow complete with two Italian ladies from Norbiton was there every Sunday morning. The ice cream was dipped out of the tub and placed on a wafer on a special holder for a wafer and it was good ice cream too when we could afford to have one.

The large house was *"The Cedars"* I think named because of the huge cedar trees in the grounds, one of which still stood years after the house was demolished. The main gate (front) looked in on the front door; all the house (was) painted black and looked very dreary along further the side or servants' entrance, as it was called in those days. A black gate and as it opened a bell hanging on a spring rang loud enough to tell them indoors that someone was about. I went in there many times as two of my aunts, my father's sisters, were

Fig 22 *The Cedars showing the back of the house facing the High Street.*

parlour maid and housemaid. Going towards the back door the usual water butt, I often had to take them mint on Sunday mornings but was never asked in. In Cedar Road there was an entrance never used in my time but could have been the entrance for a carriage. When my aunts worked there, the people who lived there were named Easton. I have been told by a friend whose father was a gardener there that a moat surrounded the garden with a drawbridge. [The Cedars *was so named after the seven cedar trees planted along the High Street about 1750 when the house was also probably built. The house and estate formed a considerable area of land, bounded to the east and west by Field Lane and Cedar Road and by the High Street and Bridgeman Road to the north and south. The house had been in the possession of the Holberton family from 1838 to 1894 and it was acquired at auction by Charles Easton in 1897. He died in 1911 and his widow departed in 1915. It was demolished in 1916].*

Along from Cedar Road, the first shop I remember was a sweet shop, Helsdons – father and mother and family; one of the sons and I walked out for a short while. Next door was the carriage repair shop owned by Mr Tomalin and his son. One could always see a trap or large wheels under repair in there. Mr Tomalin, in later years founded a town brass band. It was good too for the village fetes. Then a row of tall two storey buildings with shops in front. I remember one was an oil shop – Mr Clark, his wife and daughter. I think he is still alive and lives in Elmfield Avenue. Mr Wallis had a dyers and cleaners and in later years, very old fashioned machinery too. Mr Westwood came to Teddington with his wife and daughter and they ran a laundry reception (?). In later years Stockwell moved into a more modern shop along here. I can't remember any more before we get to the Westminster Bank on the corner of Station Road with the railway over the other side, with a field in front. *[The London County and Westminster Bank Ltd later became the National Westminster Bank plc with the merger of National Provincial Bank Ltd].*

Fig 23 *Helsdons.*

I won't go over the bridge but we'll cross over to where ***"Elmfield House"*** is. *[*Elmfield House *is one of the longest standing houses in Teddington and became the home of the Teddington Urban District Council in 1904 after a fire had burnt down the Town Hall in the Causeway in December 1903].*

Fig 24 *Elmfield House.*

Fig 25 *Teddington Fire Brigade.*

There were several large houses all occupied by noted people with the fire station just around the corner in Waldegrave Road. The fire engine was drawn by two beautiful horses and if a fire was reported and the man who drove them, had them out on the road, maybe sweeping the road, he just jumped and left everything and got back to the fire station as quickly as possible, changed into his coat and helmet and off to the fire. I don't think I ever saw such big horses race like they did back to the station as he drove the fire engine. (He) also worked for the Council.

I well remember too when there was a fire, the firemen all had a bell which sounded off in their houses. We had a fireman living quite near, after I was married in 1915 and even then they were still called to the fire by the bell. Even in the night we heard his door slam and he ran or cycled down the road half dressed and finished dressing on the fire engine racing to the fire. *[The fire engine was housed in a shed next to the Carnegie Library and the terrace of houses opposite the shed was occupied by the fire crew and their families. Automatic fire alarms were fitted to the houses].*

Fig 26 *The Carnegie Library.*

The Library, one of the first Carnegie Libraries to be erected - a marvellous thing in my early days, but when one looks back of course people of our class did not take advantage of it as one would imagine but on the other hand if one realises what opportunities we had for reading, only one lantern on the kitchen table and all the children around it. The old white kitchen table with a tapestry cloth with fringe (over it) when not in use for meals, mother in one corner sewing, my father so very often commanding silence as he did his books. He was secretary of several "slate clubs" as they were called (shared out at Christmas). We had a little homework as we got older or perhaps amusing one of the little ones with drawing (mostly with slate and pencil) or such things as noughts and crosses. Everything was amusements we made ourselves. The simplest of things would amuse us – it had to (as) we had very few toys and for hours we would cut out pictures from an old magazine. Then when bedtime came, water carried in from the scullery and a candle mostly in an enamel or tin candlestick to light one to bed.

Any lamps in the street were gas and we had the lamplighter put them on and off with the long cane and a hook, employed by the Gas Company. It was surprising too how often the gas mantles were broken. Even when years later when we moved to a new house and had gas for ages, it was wait for your father to come home and put a mantle on. I remember so well going to buy an inverted mantle and it must be Vestas.

We come back now to the High Street. There were one or two large houses – I think I'm right when I say one was ***"Teddington House"*** and ***"Tower House"*** I think the Rev. Boyd lived in, that was where our Post Office is now. The Post Office then was over the brow of the bridge towards Broad Street. *[The houses were from* Elmfield House, Percy Lodge *and* Teddington House *which became the Post Office].*

We had one very well-known fishmonger – Mr Selby. I can see the old chap now, his son followed on and lived there with his wife until they both passed away. I can't remember what was next but from then on, one or two small shops. There was a decorators – Rice and family and later there was Miles. Next came Moscrops, – Mrs Moscrop and her daughter who ran a laundry depot. I did forget to say that one of the daughters of the Rice family married my Uncle Charley, my father's youngest brother.

On the corner of Vicarage Road, Job's Dairy. I think in the early days it was Prewetts. *[These premises were a dairy since 1819. Two sisters, Louisa and Sally Barber came to Teddington and married Mr Prewett and Mr Roberts and operated the dairy there. In 1899, Louisa married her second husband, Mr Job, and continued the dairy business].* On the opposite corner I think it was an Estate Agents but I can't remember but the high class grocers was there – Coote's. The only time we were ever sent to Coote's was for bacon pieces or cracked eggs. They used to have huge wooden boxes outside each side of the doorway. Something like 4ft x 3ft

Fig 27 *Job's Dairy.*

all packed in straw so any that were cracked were put aside. We had to take a basin to get them in. About 3d bacon pieces and some cracked eggs made us a good meal. *[Milestone and Collis have been on the corner since 1890. Coote's gave way to a succession of off-licenses starting with Freddie Barratt's and ending with Wine Rack. It is currently empty, awaiting a new tenant].*

Then there were a row of houses (they are still there), they had quite big front gardens and iron fence (on wall) and iron gates. Later they built shops in front and the houses still made good dwellings because houses were really built in those days. *[All of these houses now have shops built into the front gardens. Nearly all of the houses are separate from the shops].*

Next the Miss Millards antique dealers. I spent many hours looking in their window, never understanding why some things looked like rubbish but were priced so heavily.

Fig 28 *Miss Clara Millard.*

We had the most quaint old shop next – Honeys. It belonged to the family of Honeys at the other end of the Broad Street, just demolished to make way for road widening. Well, Honey's shop sold everything. The high counter (I remember when I couldn't reach it) with glass fronted case in front and I should imagine at some previous, a stay must have put in the centre of the shop, maybe it was collapsing, for it was a pole up to the ceiling about 2½ inches in diameter and all the children just swung round it. They sold everything one could think of, from nails and screws, tools, pots and pans, paraffin and food. I don't think we ever went in for ½d biscuit crumbs without it tasted of paraffin. I really can't think of anything they didn't sell.

Then we had the side entrance to Pykes Dairies and then the little *"Tilbury Cottage"*, *The Kings Arms* and Wades Lane.

The High Street then had high trees. I should imagine a lot had gone but I so well remember one outside the *White House*, one outside Coleman's the butchers and one outside Ives side entrance. Of course the roads were not made up.

I did forget to say that the end of Vicarage Road was Ive's fields. There was a cottage inside where the caretaker or whatever he was called, lived in. (The cottage is still there). These fields went right but into three fields; the first one was where our annual fete was held, the proceeds went to the old cottage hospital in Elfin Grove. Across a second field beyond a fence and then to the next field which we called the "*Ditch Field*" for there were three ditches and we were allowed in there and when we had our school holidays we took out tea out there. Our tastes were so simple – they had to be; we had to make our own fun.

We had quite a lot though – the River, the Park and the Recreation Ground. We had very little excitement. We had no holidays. Our holidays from school were spent in Teddington and I never had a holiday in my life until well after the First World War and I was married with a son.

I heard my father say the bridge cut Teddington in half and we really had little to interest us over the other side of the bridge. *[When the railway came to Teddington in 1863, it literally cut the town in half and it took two years to construct the road bridge over the railway lines, during which people would have to go to Hampton Wick or to Strawberry Hill to cross from one side of Teddington to the other.]* They were bigger shops but they didn't seem to belong to us. It was more like going now into Kingston or Twickenham. The only time I remember going over there shopping was perhaps to the Home and Colonial on the corner or Elleray Road for two tins of condensed milk and that was when mum was getting short of cash and we could get them for 1½d a tin or a ¼lb of their butter which I think I am right in saying was 10d a pound. The poor people mostly used condensed milk. Mr Ive left his own cows and Mr Overton would come along the High Street at 4 o'clock with his covered churn to Ive's side entrance.

This may not seem a wonderful picture to many but to us older Teddingtonians, the High Street has so many real village memories. Trees lined the street. Beautiful big trees gradually getting less. The last three to go were outside the ***White House***, one outside Ive's side entrance and one outside Coleman's the butchers (where the pet shop is now in 1972 – *a Thai Restaurant is now on the same site*). You see when the railway came through, the bridge across it made the town into two separate parts; the High Street side still retained the old village atmosphere and all the old trades people were still the old village respected people.

The Broad Street had Deayton's Stores, Home and Colonial and Coffin Stores and began to develop and much more enterprising but the High Street stayed in the old ways until the shopkeepers, getting older, retired and the change came.

Fig 29 *Broad Street showing Deayton's Stores.*

Tramlines were laid and the red wood blocks laid with tar to take them. I think all of the houses smelled of tar as the pieces gathered that were chipped off, made good fuel. We would take our bags and collect as soon as we came home from school in the afternoon.

I realise that I have not mentioned one really important thing about old Teddington. Let me take you from the Westminster Bank on the corner of Station Road. Of course the railway (the British Railway) is on the right but on the left, a few houses before Christ Church. I should remember this so well for in our sitting room as children we had several models made by my father in his youth. ***"Shakespeare's Birthplace", "Ben Johnson's House"*** and a marvellous model of Christ Church which I imagine was 2ft square encased in a glass case. My father made these from small red bricks sawn out from the ordinary sized building brick but the good old red brick which he could saw into small bricks about ½ inch long and much of his material he said was cigar boxes. It *(the model)* really was perfect, front gates just as they are now in 1977, wooden and the front with trees and bushes. The belfry complete with bell. A small window at the back which had a light placed there and looking through the windows showed the pews and even the font. It was eventually given to Christ Church by my brother and is placed on a table at the back of the Church.

Fig 30 *Christchurch.*

Going on from the Church was about six houses before station gates were placed this end and another set of gates placed at the Wooden Bridge over the railway. These gates had to be closed one day each year to provide railway ownership I should imagine. Outside the station there was always a horse cab for hire. I can see the old horse now with his nose bag.

Opposite the station was a green and round the back of it, a fence from the houses which was one side of the grounds of *Gomer House*. R D Blackmore lived there until I grew up; his house was in Blackmore's Grove which turned left at the Wooden Bridge. A five bar gate half way down, one could see through to his nice old house across the lawn and further along the old black fence with the tradesmen's entrance and the usual hanging bell which rang out loudly if you touched it and of course a dog to frighten one to death. A high black tarred fence completed this with what we called Blackmore's Alley. This has memories for me as we could always go and collect Cock Horners, they seemed to like the black fence.

This enclosed the pear orchard of the most marvellous pears. This orchard stretched from Gomer Gardens right out to Udney Park Road. There was no Bolton Gardens (now built up). We used to find a hole in the black tarred fence to all the bushes on the other side. It was worth it though even if we did get chased for the William Pears could easily have each weighed 1 lb.

PART TWO

Further Recollections in 1979

[Nellie was obviously persuaded to write more about her past and whilst she does touch upon some points already covered, she brings out more information in the telling of the story and it still makes interesting reading].

A walk down memory lane in 1979.

I am now 83 years old and one of a family of eight, four boys and four girls. There are now only three of us left, I have two brothers.

My mother told me I was born in Middle Lane which is on the Broad Street side of the railway track. *(We have already covered this).*

This side (High Street) of the railway has always been our real Teddington side and all have had a great affection for our hometown and never tire of talking of old times.

Why I remember so much where I was born was because in 1915 I was married and while I was expecting my first son, I told my mother how I ate apples by the pound. She told me she was the same when she expected her first child and she just craved for apples and she said her next door neighbour gave her a pottle of apples from her garden as she had so many apple trees and even when quite green, my mother ate a pottle every day. Whether a pottle was one pound, I shall never know.

We must have moved to *Pine Cottage*, Wades Lane, off the High Street when I was very young for we lived there when I started school, for I remember Elsie Smith taking me to school because we had to cross the road. I remember being knocked down by a man on a bike. We went to Collis School, which was run by Miss Sarah Collis and afterwards by Miss May Collis. They lived together in Victoria Road, the other side of the railway. At this school the boys had to leave at ten years and go over the bridge to St Mary's and St Peter's Boys School. The girls stayed on to fourteen and then left to get work. Some who were better off stayed on to sixteen but our parents could not afford to keep us at school.

Fig 31 *St Peter & St Paul's Boys School.*

My mother's home was at Wooburn Green in Buckinghamshire. My father met her as she was in service in Kingston Road and my father lived in Hampton Wick. Our house, *Pine Cottage*, was all windows in the front. We had no back for we backed onto Ive's the butcher in the High Street. One door into our house. The sitting room door led out from there, also a door opened to the stairs which led to two bedrooms. Our scullery was about four yards from our house. The toilet and the coal shed beyond this, so we had to go outside for every drop of water. My father built a lean-to so that we could go and fill a kettle without getting soaked if it rained but to go to the toilet or get a bucket of coal, we just had a coat over our heads.

The only fireplace was in the kitchen just an open stove straight up the chimney, so you can imagine how black everything became. No heated bedrooms or sitting room. The only light was a brass oil lamp and we had to take a candle to go to bed with and in the winter, how we shivered with cold when we went to bed; our teeth chattering as we undressed. Our beds were two palliasses and a flock mattress on top. Imagine us sitting round a scrubbed wooden table with a lamp in the middle to read or write by with my mother by the fireside sewing, for she had to make most of our clothes and the boys' trousers.

I forgot to say my mother and father were married at old Wooburn Church in the 1880's. I expect their first home was in Teddington for my father was a plumber at Ham. He was known by all the old inhabitants as *"George the Plumber"*.

At that time there were some very beautiful houses there at Ham and still are now.

I remember my father telling us in the evenings, where he had been working and for whom, Admiral Fisher, Earl Dysart, Lord Beaufort, amongst others. I visited *Ham House*, once the Dysarts' place, when it was opened to the public. I remember going to Ham with my brother who was wounded in the First World War and in hospital in London. In his blue hospital uniform, we went to see my father as George had to be back at the hospital by 6 o'clock and he wanted to see dad. He was working in the dairy of one of the big houses. There were all the dairy people working and the big pans of beautiful fresh milk from the cows of their own pasture. I can hear my brother saying when we came outside "Wouldn't you think they would have given us a glass of milk." It looked so good and most of our milk at home was in tins.

My father's work on some of the houses there I could point out much of the lead work he had told us about. There was so much lead work on the roofs. He started work at 6 o'clock in the morning and always walked across Ham fields to get there. The fields then were all corn; I can see them now with all the red poppies in them. In later years, they were cultivated with vegetables - how often we pulled up a fresh carrot and ate it as we walked across.

We used to start school at four years and I can still remember the Babies Class when I first went and the teacher was Miss Balham. The seats went up in tiers so that we could all be seen by her. I often think now children who have

Fig 32 *George Joseph Chitson in his back garden at 15 Bridgeman Road.*

had so much at school to enjoy would hardly believe that. I remember that it came about that it was thought that children should have a little sport, so the boys were taken to Bushy Park for about two hours one afternoon a week. Each class went on different days. I guess they played cricket or football. Now the girls, we just went to the playground and had games such as "We'll all hold hands in a ring." I can't remember playing "Ring a ring a roses" but such games as "In and out of the windows", we would go round one at a time when you stopped in front of a girl, you took her place and she went round while we all sang. It's a job now to imagine it; it sounds so babyish but that was only once a week. Otherwise it was half an hour playing such as "Touch". One can hardly imagine it now but it's true.

We had to pay 2d a week school money. If parents were better off, they could pay more if they liked. Their names were in a special book, of course. We had I think they were called Governors of the school; perhaps two would come and just look around. I expect just to see if the school was running smoothly. One of these gentlemen was Mr Buckmaster. I know he came once and said he would like to see children save and he was going to start off one or two children in each class with a Post Office Bank Book. I guess the poorer ones were selected; I know I had one and each was given 2/6d to start it. I know I was thrilled and I tried to add to it but it wasn't easy for we only had 1d a week pocket money, so unless we earned ½d or 1d for doing errands, there was only the hope if an uncle or aunt came and it was possible to be given a penny. That sounds awful I expect but we could get sweets for 4 ozs a 1d plus 1d bar of chocolate. I wonder how many people remember Magawattee chocolate – a piece of 4 squares (very thin though) for 1d.

We had an old harmonium, which came from Collis School. My father played it and he used to bring his friends home and we would all have our special song. On Sundays my father played hymns and we would all sing. We were brought up to respect Sundays and always went to Sunday School, which was run by Miss Hobson, and then we went into St Alban's Church for the rest of the service. After Church we would dawdle around (one or two friends or my young brothers and sisters I had to care for). One thing always fascinated me was to walk around St Mary's Churchyard. I always loved the tiny pansies that grew over the graves. There was one family named Tilbury that lived in the High Street. They had a family grave there. There was a brother and sister and they had a house next door to the *King's Arms* at the bottom of Wade's Lane and when they passed away, they were buried there.

To get to our house, *Pine Cottage*, we had an alley to go up. This alley also led to the back entrance to Stacey's the chemist; next door to Ive's the butcher. At the bottom of the alley was the most old fashioned house where the Overtons lived. Old Mrs Overton was a dear little old lady. I often think this must have been something to do with a dairy for one door at the end of the alley led into a long room more like a shed and it was called *The Place*. The floor was made of slate exactly as the old slates on a roof. The grown-up lads used to have great fun but the girls were not allowed in. They (the lads) used to box each other and had lots of fun. Mr Overton was cowman to Mr Edwin G Ive, the main butcher in the High Street. He was known as the high-class butcher; all his meat was home killed.

His slaughterhouse was in Wade's Lane, a tall big-tarred building – high up were all the slats which were all open and we could hear the animals cry as they were killed. It does sound awful as I write this but we all came along with it and took very little notice of them until such times as the cowman brought up sheep or bullocks and there was no one to watch as they passed the wide slaughterhouse gate and ran on and often up the alley and into our little garden. After which all the little flowers my father had been proud of were all trampled down. I think it must have been made up to my parents in other ways for it was soon forgotten.

At the bottom of our alley was a blacksmith's shop – Mr Baltham and his assistant kept it. I used to spend a lot of time there. Many times when I was small, I was put up on the back of a big carthorse that was having new shoes on, "You stop there," they would say "then we know where you are." As I got older I would work the arm and blow the bellows for them to heat the metal to make the shoes.

Further down the lane was a big shed where there was a man who made sweets and toffee. I always thought when the doors were open it did not smell very appetising. He kept his doors shut; there were too many children about and he, evidently, didn't have patience with children as did the blacksmith.

At the top of the Lane was Smith's Orchard. When I think of the happy times I spent there with Elsie. She was my age or a little older; the one who took me to school at first. This orchard had everything; it was wonderful to me, fruit trees of all sorts. Long greenhouses with tomatoes and cucumbers, huge potting sheds and one thing I see in my mind's eye at the moment, a great big mulberry tree. I can see Mr Smith now with a round punnet in one hand with a big mulberry in the bottom and filling it with big luscious mulberries. I guess there are heaps of people who have never tasted one. These were special and were only picked for orders for the rich people on Broom Road, and of course, very expensive. In fact that was the only mulberry tree I knew of with the exception of one in a house just off the orchard in Vicarage Road only separated by a wall, and owned by Mr Sam Spring and his son and daughter, Dick and Rose. Sam was stone deaf and a friend of my father. I might add that where his house was is now the Teddington Swimming Baths.

We now will go to the High Street end of Wade's Lane. One corner was the *King's Arms* Public House owned by Mr Barnes and son and wife. This was a beer house open all day, the bars with sloping fronts and sawdust on the floors. Just forms (benches) to sit on. I used to take the son's children out when I grew up a bit; Pamela and Boswick was the baby boy and a very sick child too. I can see the pram I was so proud to push – pale blue with wickerwork all over it. I wonder if people could picture that now. This little boy died young and I know how sad I was although I knew he was very weak.

PART THREE

Family and Other Recollections in 1981

[Again Nellie was persuaded to relate more of her past and this time concentrated on her own family. In particular we learn something of her husband, Tom and his family.

The Stocker family were farm workers in Hampshire from the late 1600s to the 1880s when this line of the family moved to South West London. In 1882 Thomas Lorenzo Stocker moved to Balham where he worked in his uncle's barge building business at Frogmore Wharf, Wandsworth. His son Thomas was born in 1886. In 1900 the family moved to 3 Gomer Gardens in Teddington and young Thomas started a seven year apprenticeship with Robert Neale Tough of Tough & Henderson at Teddington Lock. In 1907, Thomas senior moved back to Wandsworth to take over his late uncle's business. At that time, Thomas junior was in Teddington Cottage Hospital with rheumatic fever. When he came out, he found that his apprenticeship had been extended by a year.

He married Nellie on 15th September 1915 at Kingston Registry Office.

Also, although out of the Edwardian era, we find out about some of the charity work that Nellie was involved in and which was clearly a forerunner to our present Silver Threads and Community Care Groups.]

I have written so many times of the old days, mostly because of the vast difference in life today. It's a different world now in 1981 and I have reached the age of 85. I seem to go as far as being married to a fine man and having two sons.

I must go back a little though to say a word or two of my husband, Tom.

He came from a family of barge builders, for in those days barge transport was very important for the barges carried goods up the Thames, loaded with all sorts of important cargo. There were no cars of any sort on the roads then. Living at Teddington, it was a real sight to see huge great loaded barges going through Teddington Lock, heading to Kingston Wharves with coal, timber, food and many other things. *[River transport was the principle way in which goods were moved in those days and the Thames highway was always very busy].*

The wharf was where my husband worked as a lad. His father and a friend who owned the yard did repairs on damaged barges. Opposite this yard were great warehouses (they were at the end of a canal at Wandsworth). One old firm I remember so well – Pease's Wharf, where barges were unloaded with corn and all sorts of things I can't remember. Also Tate & Lyle Wharf – these two companies were opposite Stocker's Yard and when the War was on, it was most fortunate for all working there if a bag of sugar should burst while unloading for this was shovelled up as it was rationed during the War. Often there were little dark bits in it but it was very useful.

My evenings were spent sometimes listening to things Tom used to tell me.

Attached to the yard through all the store of wood and equipment was a huge high shed through a gate up a yard to two houses where Tom's family lived, quite a space and the partner's house.

Tom had several brothers and sisters: Maud, Charlotte, Rose and Olive were the girls; Charley, Tom, Fred, Harry, Arthur and Cecil the boys.

In those early days, they pottered in the yard. When Tom was ten years old (1896), his father came to Teddington to the world famous Barge Builders Yard of Robert Neale Tough, the originator of the now "Tough Brothers" about three or four generations back. He had to wait until he was old enough to be apprenticed. He served seven years apprenticeship with Robert Tough and he was the only apprentice that Robert Tough had. He lived at Barnes and he was very proud of Tom and if he had a job at his own house that needed doing, he always asked for Tom Stocker. He didn't ever want anyone else. *[Robert Neal Tough was running the Blackfriars yard of Tough & Henderson whilst his brother,*

Arthur, was running the Teddington yard. Arthur did not take to the business and left to form his own coal merchants. His sons Douglas and Gordon formed the present firm of Tough Brothers Ltd in 1922]

Tom was a clever man, he (Robert Tough) always said in later years when motors came into being. Tom learned everything for then tugs were more

Fig 33 *Tom Stocker and Nellie Chitson before they were married at the front of 15 Bridgeman Road.*

mechanised and he said he could lay down the keel and build a boat himself. He could install an engine and do all the electrical parts to fit out a tug after it was built. *[In 1909/10, Tom went to an evening class at Battersea Polytechnic and took a course on car mechanics and driving. For a number of years, he drove cars for a living; he drove actors who lived in Teddington back and forth to the London theatres for their performances. He went back to barge building in 1924, moving into boat building with Robert Tough in 1928].*

In the early days I well remember him coming home very dirty and tired. A barge had been built and before all the flimsy things could be done to it, it had to be blacked. Hot tar over heat had to be put all over the outside with long handled brushes. The black smoke from that process got into everything. Of course this was after they had been all over it with caulking tools, tapping special twisted cotton caulking in the joints between the planks so that the boat was completely watertight.

Tom took great pride in any work he did. Pride of work was a great thing in those days for Tom was the same type of man as my father. If he did a job, you know it was done properly. Many years after if there was a shed or anything Tom had erected, there was always the remark "I know who put this up" for it was harder to get down than expected. It was made to last. I still have a small round table; you can sit on it and I don't think you'll ever find that it will fall to pieces. It's very sturdy. I would not part with it although when he made, I remember him saying "It's not much good" as it was made with wood he had at home.

He was very fond of sport especially football. I went with him to Chelsea or Fulham as they were at home on alternative Saturdays. I also went with him when we went to see the Kingstonians or Casuals for they were at home on alternative Saturdays too. *[Both clubs shared a ground on the Richmond Road, Kingston, which has sadly given way to new housing]*

Another sport he loved to watch was cricket and our Sunday walk in the summer was to see Teddington play cricket in Bushy Park. In those days there were two teams - The Gents and Teddington Town. They both had a good following but as usual in the old days, class distinction was rife and the Gents were always considered a cut above Teddington Town which consisted of the town workmen. *[Teddington Cricket Club used to play on the green where Teddington Railway Station now stands and moved to new premises in Bushy Park in 1863. They played on Saturdays and Sundays. Teddington Town Cricket Club was originally formed as St Peter and St Paul's Cricket Club and consisted of the shopkeepers and tradesmen and played on Wednesdays {the traditional local half day} and Sundays. There is still some rivalry between the two].*

Our two boys were sporty too. Wal was always much more for watching sport than Jack, he enjoyed his fun with his friends more. Wal loved tennis and played a lot of very good players too. When Wimbledon Tennis was on, Wal had his annual holiday so that he could spend a lot of time there if possible. People cannot possibly appreciate what a boon TV is, to be able to sit at home and see these so well. Wal played cricket and football for Leyland Motors and he once took a team of footballers to Leyland Motors and captained the team there.

Mrs Read was a marvellous person. I am sure she must always have had the welfare of old people at heart.

When I first knew her, her husband was alive although he was quite a bit older than herself, she always kept him interested in her projects. In the early days before I knew her, she organised a Grandfathers' Club. It was held in a little hall of sorts in Queens Road. *[There was a small hall in Queens Road for many years. It seems to have been built as a blacksmiths but later became an entertainments hall and cinema]*. Eventually a committee was formed and I was of the opinion that Mrs Read must have had it in mind for a long time to try and make up an organisation for both sexes of elderly people, who were needy, lonely or sick for when I came into the organisation, a committee had been formed and consisted of really dedicated people interested in old folk and at that time, there were a great number of folk in their seventies and many were poor and in need.

In fact in my area the number was surprisingly high when one began to enquire. They obtained the use of ***Craig Hall*** in Clarence Road *[This was an old municipal building which had served as the first Methodist Church in Teddington and later became a magistrate's court]* for people who were able to get there for five open afternoons a week for a cup of tea and cake. The helpers took it in turns to make cakes. They would knit or sew and play cards or dominoes. Once a month a tea and entertainment was announced at the Baptist Hall for folk of sixty-five or over. The Baptist Church allowed us to use their hall so that many who couldn't get there were brought by volunteer car drivers. For many of them, this was the only outing they had.

We eventually had to make the age group seventy years because the Hall would not hold them all. The Committee was represented by all local organisations: the Townswomen's Guild, all churches and chapels in the town, the Salvation Army and the Red Cross. The Committee had sub-committees for catering, outings, and a visiting register. We met once a month to report. We were well organised with Chairman, Vice -Chairman, Secretary, Treasurer and a good committee. They spared no effort to find ways to get funds. The incumbents of S.T. *(whoever they were)* paid 1/- (one shilling) a year and we held jumble sales, whist drives and once a year, all the shopkeepers were asked for a small donation or gift to run a Christmas Bazaar and we had a nice successful raffle at the same time.

My work in those days was visiting. I visited along with as many visitors as we could get voluntarily to try and see the old folk who were unable to get out or were alone and lonely. People were not so well off in the early days and we helped out with gifts when visiting from organisational funds and many times we found folk with not enough coal or bedding and helped them out. We had a fund we could call on, if anything was beyond our working funds. At that time and still now we would find the chief trouble is loneliness. They are better cared for now than in the early days and can get more help but now that women go to work, there are not so many women able to do visiting. I have for many years been Visiting Secretary and have visitors who have visited Homes and Hospitals where we have our old folk and they do a marvellous job.

Of course we now have *Elleray Hall.* This was once a church hall, an entertainments hall and an engineering shop. One of our committee saw the possible opportunity, when it became empty, to make it a hall for our old folk. It was in an awful condition as one can imagine but with a little help from the Borough Council and a good deal of hard work and planning, we now have a nice hall for folk to have a cheap daily meal and company, run by a very efficient manager and committee and again very helpful volunteers. [Elleray Hall *is named after an old house that stood off North Lane. It is recorded on the O/S map of 1863/4 but had gone by 1893/4 when the next map was published. The Hall is shown on the next map of 1915 and is still in use today as the main premises of the Silver Threads Association, a community care group with its emphasis on the elderly].*

Poems

Nellie was also given to writing poetry and here are some of her compositions

When you're arthritic, rheumatic, the lot,
Pain every morning in each joint you've got.
Oh what an effort, you've had a bad night
Whatever your thoughts, nothing seems right.
You make the effort with stick, crutch or frame,
A nice cup of tea and life won't seem the same.
You get washed and dressed to start off the day,
Perhaps there's a visitor calling your way.
To think someone in passing would knock on your door,
And ask how you were; could you really ask more.
Maybe their kindness will not ease the pain
But give them encouragement to call in again.
For one never knows what they may endure,
They will seldom tell you, of that I am sure.
It's often one that has less time to spare
That remembers the lonely and ones that need care.
So as you age, don't let yourself go
Keep up your chin and let everyone know.
You're as old as you feel, not as old as you look.
Age comes from inside, not from grey locks.
I know it's not easy to smile when in pain
But crying don't help, so smile just the same.

Think of the folk in chairs on TV
Paraplegics they called them, wonderful to see
How they played hockey and tennis as happy could be
When they tried hard to walk so determinedly
But their lives depend on the way they make it
They exercise harder to keep themselves fit.
So don't sit and brood and think all is gloom
For nice thoughts can improve so much in a room.
You must have faith and feel someone's near
You'll know then for certain there's nothing to fear.

Life is not easy as we all know
Problems encountered – the spirit gets low.
For in each day there is something to learn,
Some fresh thoughts of which way to turn.
A smile from a neighbour, a thought from a friend,
So much for so little, a lot will depend.
A call on one lonely to give them fresh thought
Does much more good than a gift you have brought.
To give just a lift from a dreary mind
Is work such a lot as you will find
Not only lonely but perhaps cannot see
A book not that comfort as with you or me.
So if you have a few minutes to spare,
Find someone alone that few minutes to share.
Maybe they'll see no one else for that day,
Their mind retains thought of something you say.
Then comes the night when they lie down in bed
A smile on their face over something you said.

In Bushy Park I picture the trees
So stately, erect, defying the breeze.
The Chestnut Avenue, a mile in length
A stretch of glory and wonderful strength.
I've seen the boughs beaten when north winds blow
And seen them all heavy with white winter snow.
Then in the spring, the boughs start to wake,
The bumps where shortly the shoots start to break.
Then come the sticky buds all bronzy and brown,
With just a small colour of red golden crown.
All the long winter the sturdy strong roots
Sucking up moisture to prepare for the shoots.
Then when the leaves begin to spread green,
Ready for flowers that soon will be seen.
They grow up like a cone and sit on the leaves
Taking no notice as the wind huffs and heaves.
Later the petals will cover the ground,
You'll soon see the pimply balls that abound.
The children watching as they grow big and strong
Enough to play conkers all the day long.
The deer and the stags search on the ground
For those that all fallen and lying around.
Their feed of conkers and acorns each season
Supply a big need and a very good reason.
For it's time for the deer and stags to prepare
For the little fawns later in their home to share.
So are the children alive to do best
A conker on string and a friend to contest.

APPENDIX 1

Nellie Stocker's Teddington High Street 1905

Elmfield House
(Percy Lodge)
➢ *Elmfield Avenue*
Teddington House
Tower House (?)
Mr Selby - Fishmonger
2 shops/houses
Mr Rice & Family - Decorators
Mr Miles
Mrs Moscrop - Laundry
Jobs Dairy
➢ *Vicarage Road*
Estate Agents (Milestone & Collis)
St Mary's Vicarage
Messrs Coote's - High Class Grocers
3 shops/houses
Miss Millard - Antique dealer
Messrs Honey's - Grocers
Pykes Dairy
Westminster Bank
12 shops/houses
Mr Stockwell - Cycles
Mr Westwood - Laundry
Mr Wallis - Dyers Cleaners
Mr Clark - Oil Shop
Mr Tomalin - Carriage Repairs
Messrs Helsdons - Sweet Shop
➢ *Cedar Road*
The Cedars
➢ *Field Lane*
The White House, the Doctors' House
Jewellers (J H Jones)
Messrs Pouparts - Dairy
Mr Millest - Baker
Messrs Russells - Drapers (double)
Mr Norrish - Grocer
Messrs Coleman & Sons - Butcher
small field

Tilbury Cottage
Kings Arms PH
- ➢ *Wades Lane*

Mr & Mrs Glue - Sweetshop
Tailor
Draper
Barber's shop
- ➢ *Steps*

Mr Stacey - Chemist
Mr E G Ive - High Class Butcher
Mr Chester - Decorator
Mr Tozer - Baker
- ➢ *Watts Lane*

Mrs Mayhew - Greengrocer
Mr Cleak - Toyshop
Fishmonger - (Walter Preece)
Messrs Porters - Undertakers
4 other shops/houses
Mr Beaney - Boot Shop
Kings Head PH
Horse Cab Yard
- ➢ *Cambridge Road*

Mr Tait - Dentist
3 other houses
(Club)
6 other houses
(Oak Cottage)
Mr Metcalf - Corn Chandler
Peg Woffington Cottages

Bridgeman House - St Albans Club
Mr Stockwell - Cycles
Mr Lemon - Baker
2 shops
- ➢ *Udney Park Road*

Grand Parade
Block of flats with shops below
- ➢ *Kingston Lane*

Mr Metcalf - Corn Chandler
2 shops/houses
Royal Oak PH
Mr Morgan - Sweet shop
Messrs Pomfretts - Hire Carriages
Old Cottages
St Albans Adult School
- ➢ *Langham Road*

St Albans Church

APPENDIX 2

Kelly's Directory of Teddington High Street 1905

Elmfield House
Ephraim Davis
- *Elmfield Avenue*

James Selby - Fishmonger
Mrs M Morris - Antique Dealer
William Rice & Sons - Builders/Undertakers
Sydney William Rice
Miss Annie Moscrop - Registry for Servants
Ernest Pennington - Auctioneer
H A Job - Dairy
- *Vicarage Road*

Milestone & Collis - Auctioneers
Miss Millard - Antique Dealer
Thomas Coote - Grocer
Miss Clara Millard - Antique Dealer
Wm John Honey - Oilman
Ernest Martin Jn - Boot Man.
Pyke Brothers - Dairymen
Miss Tilbury
Westminster Bank
Charles Robert Lancashire
Chas Sirrell - Ironmonger
Fred N Crabbe - Stationer
Stockwell & Sons - Cycles
Wm Clapham Jn - Tailor
Premium Trading Stamp Co.
Robert E Evans - Milliner
Miss Miriam Mann - Refreshments
Mrs L Ouseley - Ferndale Laundry
Rays Royal Registries
Clarence Lake - Fruiterer
Herbert's Meat Stores
Richard Frickert - Hairdresser
Wm J Davis - Oil & Color Man
R Langston-Jones - Electrical Engs
Fredk Wm Tomalin & Son - Coach Bl
Mrs M M Watt - Confectioner
- *Cedar Road*

Kings Arms PH

- *Wades Lane*

George Tuck - Tobacconist
Walter Preece - Fishmonger
Peter Casey - Chemist
Edwin George Ive - Butcher
Thomas Emmett
James Hyatt & Sons - Plumbers
Thomas Woodford & Sons - Bakers

- *Watts Lane*

Thomas Robert Brown - Greengrocer
Cyril Cleak - Stationer
George Hy Rudd - Dentist
Mrs Mary French - China & Glass
Herbert Horwill - Confectioner
Marguerite - Blouse Specialist
Wm Porter Jn - Undertaker
Arthur & Co - Printers
Mrs Messenger
Edward Beaney - Boot Man
Kings Head PH
Frederick Wm Bowdidge - Jobmaster

- *Cambridge Road*

Arthur M Fox - Dentist
Harold Pearson Tait - Dentist
Alexander Reynolds Cripps - Solicitor
Arthur Vine
Miss Mary Scott - Boarding House
Henry Archibald Hinton
Mrs Dade
Mrs Wright
Miss A H Kirk - School
George West - Tailor (Oak Cottage)
William George Sale
Mrs Huggins
Henry Bishop
Mrs Georgina S Hatcher - News Agent
Miss Millard - show grounds
The Cedars - Mrs Easton

- *Field Lane*

The White House, the Doctors' House
Parr's Bank Ltd
J H Jones - Watch Maker
W Poupart & Son - Dairymen
Chas John Millest - Baker
Telephone Exchange
William Perryman Russell - Draper
Rush Brothers - Grocers
James P Coleman - Butcher
Bridgeman House - St Albans Club
H J Graham & Co - Wine Merchant
Charles Edward Lemon - Baker
Frederick Wm Bowdidge - Jobmaster

- *Udney Park Road*

A Pixton - Furniture Dealer
Model Court Laundry
John C Hill & Co - Estate Agents
Sirrell Bros - Tailors
Saving Stamp Co
Chas E Hudson - Hair Dresser
Sydney Cookson - Confectioner
Star Wine Co
C A E Cordle - Picture Frame Maker
Saunders & Co - Motor & Cycle Wks

- *Kingston Lane*

Miss F M Pearson - Fruiterer
James Edward Metcalf - Corn Chand. & Post Office
Misses G & S Rice - Stationers
William Woodard - Coffee Rooms
Royal Oak PH
Bertie Green - Boot Maker
Edwd Heather - Cab Proprietor
William Pomfrett - Fly Proprietor
Jas Morgan - Tobacconist
J C Clark - Shopkeeper
Teddington Adult School (St Albans)

- *Langham Road*

INDEX